EPIGRAMS AT LARGE

EPIGRAMS AT LARGE

Fred J. Singer

PHILOSOPHICAL LIBRARY
New York

ENDOWMENT

Throughout a basic conscience one gleans those truths which, when analyzed magnanimously, generate sentiments of indebtedness to a single individual.

I therefore seek the readers' indulgence in pausing with me briefly as these words are offered in dedication to my dear friend William S. Abrams, M.S., L.S., Librarian at Portland State College, Portland, Oregon, for his comments and encouragement at inception, during the writing, and upon completion of this book.

THE AUTHOR

PROLOGUE

No thought ever formulated is unique
unto itself; just a new drape on an old
framework.

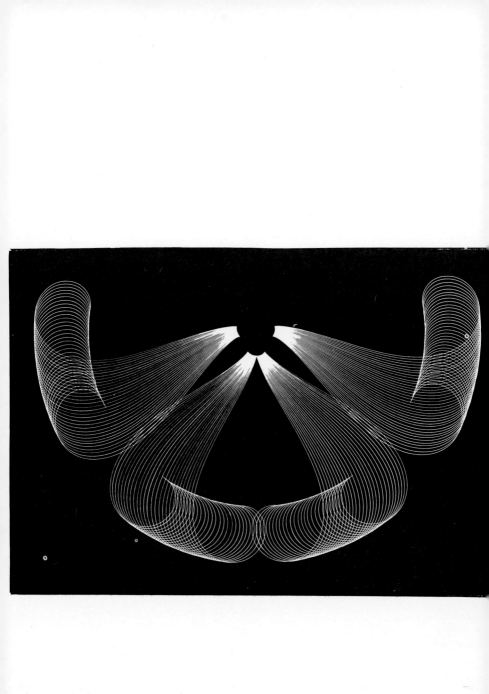

Burning, Ashes, by
    Offenses;
Turning, Smashes, my
    Defenses.

Affray, Agress, tease
    Tormenting;
Defray, Regress, ease
    Relenting.

FOREWORD

Most people have a sufficiently burdensome load to carry of their own to concern themselves with. They do not, as a rule, choose to be afflicted with inscrutable, pedantic philosophical treatises to muddle through at length.

In truth, philosophy en masse can be likened to classic music—only the most popular, or the easiest to recall, are well liked. Therefore, the ensuing jottings, which have enjoyed favorable commentaries from friends in a number of previews, may prove to be somewhat more agreeable on your digestive tracts.

It is at the suggestion of those of my friends who were exposed to it that I decided to submit my manuscript to the publishers. However, my gratitude goes to my wife, without whose help this would never have materialized.

FRED J. SINGER

SYNOPSIS OF COMPONENTS:

a. The Gist,

                relieved by

b. Some Verse,

                interspersed by

c. Art in Op,

                followed by

    More Gist

                ended by

    Less Help

GLOSSARY OF AUGMENTATIONS

	Art	Names of: *Poems*
Frontispiece	Feathercurls	Plaint
Page 20	Vertigo	Man
28	Quints	Graphics
34	Progression	Scars
40	Rotor	Constancy
48	Offsetting	Retrospect
54	Steps	Thoughtlessness
62	Burst	Birth
68	Concentric	Dawn
74	Fusion	Prerequisites
80	Ecstasy	Paintings
90	Maelstrom	Beginning
Backpiece	Codicil	

by the Author

. . . The statues of clay at whose pedestal we fall, themselves come tumbling in time . . .

. . . Mirrors are liars, and liars don't mirror . . .

. . . A step in reverse requires two ahead to go forward . . .

. . . One builds a castle for oneself and then promptly becomes its prisoner . . .

. . . Complacency robs one of initiative . . .

. . . Everyone loves a lover, except the unloved . . .

. . . The anomalous themes of variation mesmerize the males enfolded by the arms of The Milo . . .

. . . Sacrifice is selflessness gone sour in the name of glory . . .

. . . The spring of misery feeds the river of tears . . .

. . . Enter money, exit dignity . . .

. . . Self-sufficiency is independence graduating cum laude . . .

. . . Bad pennies don't turn up, they are made . . .

. . . The deepest wounds don't bleed . . .

. . . Full stomachs know not hunger . . .

. . . The strongest shackles bind us to convention . . .

. . . At least one membrane in each vocal cord bears the legend 'Hot Air' . . .

. . . Mores breathe their last as lust breathes its first . . .

. . . To remain poor, disdain the mile after being handed the inch . . . .

17

. . . A human being is not always being human . . .

. . . Dogmas impose . . .

. . . Demand nothing, and never get it . . .

. . . The haves prey on the have-nots . . .

. . . Of all the mighty pillars of society, the stoutest one occupies the central position—money . . .

. . . The 'rat race' is something even the rats do not participate in . . .

. . . Those who are ground into the dust will stay there till they grow up . . .

. . . It is hard enough thinking what you are. Now try being what you are . . .

. . . Self is to being as bark is to tree . . .

. . . Trees are green to all except the color-blind . . .

. . . Interest precedes intent . . .

. . . Conflicting ideologies are necessary evils; they stimulate economies . . .

. . . Conservation is exercised by hunting whilst wars conserve the hunter . . .

. . . Without receiver; no broadcast . . .

. . . Home is where the mind is, not where you hang your hat . . .

. . . Nocturnal activities go on around the clock . . .

. . . Don't do it, and the world slips by . . .

. . . If you like needles, be darned . . .

. . . 'To be, or not to be' is not the question; it is the fact . . .

. . . Across the face of history march we, unlovely . . .

. . . In a world of Amazons, men are slaves though they were not told . . .

. . . No two peas in a pod are alike . . .

. . . Bank accounts do stretch, with rubber checks . . .

. . . Most interest around is in self . . .

. . . The principled are restricted; the bigoted are frightened; the existentialist is unsure . . .

. . . If legs can't move, minds will . . .

. . . A lift in the States is not a ride in England. Conversely, to be taken for a ride here is unlike being taken up an English lift . . .

. . . The law is 'strange': You can't live with it, you can't live without it. You watch it, it watches you. Big brother watches you, and big brother is you . . .

. . . The sexes are not so much opposite, as opposed . . .

. . . See a face all puckered up and you'll know its owner drives a lemon . . .

. . . Overcome fear in death . . .

. . . Emulate another and lose self . . .

. . . Those who say 'no ifs, ands or buts about it' believe in the power of positive thinking . . .

. . . The body is just an instrument, a vehicle for the mind . . .

. . . Determine your net essence and then, undiluted, commit it in gainful engagement . . .

. . . Coercion is a powerful moving force. However persuasion is better . . .

. . . Don't just stand there—exist! . . .

There he was!
Man, full-blown.
Knew no cause;
Effect unknown.

Here he is
Man, all dazed.
Truth not his
Stares amazed.

. . . Lambaste—you're a nihilist. Engage and you're a humanist . . .

. . . No death is as great as that of hope . . .

. . . Any credo is good, so long as adhered to . . .

. . . Humanitarianism is the heart, magnanimity its blood . . .

. . . When we die our works live on for a period of time dependent upon the number of people who believed in those 'works' . . .

. . . Throw off repression, and you experience blinding, intense exhilaration . . .

. . . Those who rely in self, need an idol . . .

. . . One of anything is unique and priceless. Two or more of the same becomes commonplace . . .

. . . True love is an extremely short-lived commodity, with the majority . . .

. . . Be anything but blasé . . .

. . . To be happy is to be unencumbered . . .

. . . Habitual honesty is stepped on . . .

. . . In all which is contagious, consider courage . . .

. . . Defy the world and you'll fail yourself . . .

. . . Self-discipline is a form of hypnosis . . .

. . . Sublime ambition is a key to wealth . . .

. . . The one who has 'everything' is from that moment forth destitute . . .

. . . True freedom is non-existent . . .

. . . The word 'unattainable' has never lived up to its definition . . .

. . . Originality is a journey into the unknowable . . .

. . . Try taking more than you receive, if you can . . .

. . . All that which is labeled has been had . . .

. . . The bereaved are fortified, but never immune . . .

. . . Illusions metamorphose into disillusionment . . .

. . . Good intentions do not pave the road to hell; circumstances do . . .

. . . Begging is like flattery, it gets you nowhere . . .

. . . Squallor is a disease. Luckily, it can be cured . . .

. . . A good substitute will have outlived its usefulness the moment its original appears . . .

. . . Tolerance is good; Acceptance is better; Participation is best . . .

. . . For wont of anything better to do, be involved . . .

. . . Teaching someone a single thing makes the world a richer place . . .

. . . Set the world afire, you're in the public eye; be a conformist, you're a nonentity . . .

. . . One honesty sometimes begets another . . .

. . . Blinded eyes are replaced by active hands . . .

. . . The absolute is unattainable . . .

. . . How to please customers in numerous, heart-breaking lessons . . .

. . . Give in just a little, and the ball of surrender will start rolling . . .

. . . If all customers were king, the world would have no peons . . .

. . . When there is nothing left to give, one must needs receive . . .

. . . No democrat is entirely democratic in a democracy, nor anywhere else . . .

. . . A great man once said, "Give me liberty, or give me death." The latter will come to us as it did to him. Where is liberty? . . .

. . . Even thick skulls can be penetrated . . .

. . . Of all the asinine questions to ask anyone, try 'what is life?' . . .

. . . Words without actions are just that . . .

. . . The moment one says 'but' a giant step is taken—backwards . . .

. . . The one who has tasted neither the heights nor pits is among the living dead . . .

. . . Controlling your anger, though civilized, thwarts your expression of a natural prerogative . . .

. . . Sophistication is not solely reserved for the rich . . .

. . . Even the blind can 'see' . . .

. . . Interdependencies are inextricable . . .

. . . 'Nowhere' is a neutral ground . . .

. . . Progress is escalation of frenzy . . .

. . . The highest price tag of them all must be affixed to human character; whatever remains of it, that is . . .

. . . The tyranny of words has now merged with its staunchest ally to mop up recalcitrant stragglers to the campaign in favor of abject enslavement—NUMBERS . . .

. . . Though you strive till every bone in your body cracks, yet will you never quite be able to rise above yourself . . .

. . . A spy is a gossip who can keep his mouth shut . . .

24

. . . Tragedy is unwanted offspring . . .

. . . Within the human mind, the presence of two titans at variance are inescapably irreconcilable—Idealism and Materialism . . .

. . . An adage is a distilled thought . . .

. . . Be committed, or waste away in drab despair . . .

. . . Conventionality rules supreme . . .

. . . Women are perennially laboring to romanticize life clear out of cognizance . . .

. . . The skeletons of dreams lie scorching on the desert of disappointment . . .

. . . Parades, fanfare and forceful oratory—all insiduously devilish and ingenious, psychological devices for mass stimulation, or to beat a goggle-eyed, overflowing populace into a pulp, or their minds inspired to legalized killing . . .

. . . Selfishness runs deeper than you think . . .

. . . Contemporary degeneracy is of heart . . .

. . . Of all minds one might attempt to convert, the flexible is the most difficult . . .

. . . Oftentimes turbulent waters run over a chasm . . .

. . . The frozen valves to the adrenal ducts are called self-control . . .

. . . If you are not awake, no one bothered to arouse you . . .

. . . Skeletal dreams in need of flesh are dreamed with eyes wide open . . .

. . . The stage of the world has no audience . . .

. . . Those of few words do not generally become ingredients in a soup. They usually eat it . . .

. . . If actors are made rather than born, most makers failed to inspect their product . . .

. . . The blessed are the non-afflicted, and the lucky who stay that way . . .

. . . The least known is also in pitiful disuse—empathy . . .

. . . Hope has wreathes placed on it . . .

. . . Rigidity is compatibility's greatest enemy . . .

. . . Marriage is a sweet estate in an unnatural state . . .

. . . The proverbial pistol poised at your head, was placed there by you . . .

. . . Given an honest choice between death and running, the world is apt to see a neat pair of heels . . .

. . . Search and you shall never find a real non-coward . . .

. . . The depths of fear cannot be plumbed . . .

. . . Misgivings are odors of pending trouble. Smell 'em? . . .

. . . That which is the gentlest, is also the most vulnerable . . .

. . . The longest list of any falls right under the word "shortcomings" . . .

. . . People are so full of holes, it's a marvel they can keep anything inside . . .

. . . If everyone wrote, few would read . . .

. . . Ecstasy in search of woman . . .

. . . We are no less and we are no more. This can be found somewhere in a constitution . . .

. . . Any constitution could never transcend the constituents who constituted it . . .

. . . Atmosphere is like a woman's dress—skirts the main issue . . .

. . . Do you rule words, or are you ruled by them? Here's fuel for the fire: just grapple with the definition of the word 'unthinkable' . . .

. . . When you applaud a performing dog, whom is it directed at? The trainer? Poor devil, he needs it to reaffirm his supremacy . . .

. . . If you are out to win an arms race, just bite a dog. That's the canine's only weapon . . .

. . . A word is forever . . .

. . . Recall of anything is as futile as absolution. The advantage of the latter, however, is manifest: there are repeats . . .

. . . To be excommunicated, do anything to excess . . .

. . . Be different, you're an eccentric. Try a little harder, you are 'bad.' And should you relish solitude, give it all you've got . . .

. . . Those who feel sorry for you, forget their troubles in yours . . .

. . . Laziness is the mother of uselessness . . .

. . . Man barges through life establishing dependencies . . .

. . . Where brain fails, brawn steps in . . .

. . . Show me one failure and I'll show you his gloating successor . . .

. . . If you don't wish to be stepped on, don't fall down . . .

. . . Hold out your hand for help and expect to retrieve it, empty . . .

. . . Perfume usurps other nauseous offenders . . .

Sweet is the luxury
    Of the mighty pen;
Dear now the liberty
    In unbiased ken.
Might not its verity
    Fill all hungered yen?
Spill forth its subtlety
    To all candid men?

The power in the ink:
    Quiet, tender, soft—
Rush through the minds which think;
    Perch on stars aloft.
Words from hands, one sly wink
    To all thought will waft
The key and only link.
    These—not stressed too oft.

. . . When the words 'The Lord helps the one who helps himself' were given, that's all you got . . .

. . . The need for mastery is an inherent weakness . . .

. . . Dueling fathered competition. One would prefer the former; at least you faced your adversary . . .

. . . Seduction is bedazzlement, at which the peacock excels . . .

. . . If embryos could foretell, they might abort . . .

. . . Normalcy is akin to the average. The former cannot be, whilst the latter is merely a mythical cypher . . .

. . . The less one sleeps, the longer one stretches the inevitable . . .

. . . It is hard to see the truths for all the lies . . .

. . . Finality rests in repose . . .

. . . Staples overcome loyalties . . .

. . . Real need is regal . . .

. . . Countries without a King have more than one queen . . .

. . . To win is glory; to lose is human . . .

. . . Pure thought is impure . . .

. . . An attempt to complete any single statement would deplete all available paper stock on earth before so much as the surface is scratched . . .

. . . There is nothing which does not leave a great deal to be desired . . .

. . . The only consolation we have is that there will always be 'something' . . .

. . . The strangest word in the dictionary is 'nothing.' Since thoughts are things, even thinking it embodies something . . .

. . . Some logicians there are who experience difficulty with the multiplication table . . .

. . . No known downfall was ever so great as to elude the archeologist, so watch your step . . .

. . . To learn what we can from past mistakes, would leave no time for current ones. The future bloopers must fend for themselves . . .

. . . When someone says 'you are on your own,' it is not very newsworthy . . .

. . . Expressions (figures of speech) are indigenous to their eras . . .

. . . There is no triumph greater than victory over vengeance . . .

. . . Pacifism is reserved for the civilized . . .

. . . When we have refined oil flowing through our veins, then will we also be completely civilized. The sadness is that heart will be missing . . .

. . . The most poignant example of self-indoctrination is the concept of life in the hereafter. A better one, hopefully . . .

. . . The clock stops only for lovers . . .

. . . Some say that life is both a farce and a sham. Be that as it may, it's the only one we've got . . .

. . . If there is a bona fide miracle, it is the unswerving belief in a second existence, only this time eternal . . .

. . . To remove all of us who are pagans would remove all criteria from the devout . . .

. . . All values fluctuate like the dickens. The weeding out occurs, usually, when one is too old to enjoy them . . .

. . . Chagrin is awakened when ego is injured . . .

. . . The promiscuous live in fear of exposure. If they could just keep their clothes on . . .

. . . Daylight whitewashes the exertions of the dark . . .

. . . Physical bents possess no magnetism—just gravity . . .

. . . If that which is bad were taken away, values of 'good' would undergo a cataclysmic reduction . . .

. . . Spiritual attraction does not have the outlet as does the physical. That is why it lasts longer . . .

. . . The smallest, the mightiest and the most sinister building block of all time is the human sperm . . .

. . . What the menace which is man touches—withers . . .

. . . Cry out in pain to a deaf world . . .

. . . Love often needs glasses, but the lovers don't wear them . . .

. . . Greatness comes with diligent practice . . .

. . . The offspring of an Einstein, if left in the veldt, would become a helpless aborigine . . .

. . . Inhibition through discipline . . .

. . . Most ethics are based on near, or half, truths . . .

. . . A half-truth is surpassed by an honest lie . . .

. . . Incongruity: written of, but not explained . . .

. . . Injustice multiplies itself . . .

. . . Should Euclid have met Einstein, his rigidity would bend . . .

. . . If even the specific mass and electric charge of a single atom fluctuates, how can an entire galaxy of them within the human system possibly be stable? . . .

. . . Digressors, in their actions and non-action, serve to re-assure the staid, ingrained propriety of the righteous, but not without covert winsomeness . . .

. . . Censure throttles free choice . . .

. . . Strictness is a precept under any banner of belief . . .

. . . The more an ethic diverges off an accepted norm, the more its devotees are censured . . .

. . . No one human being, nor a million, can pass judgment on a single kindred spirit with incontrovertible equity; beyond the shadow of fallible doubt; without the vestige of inevitable bias . . .

. . . Footloose and fancies poor . . .

. . . Beasts are feared because of their naturalness—a plane to which we may never aspire . . .

. . . Honor among the carnivorous is the conscience we dream of . . .

. . . Guilt belongs to those who decry it . . .

. . . 'There's a Joker in every deck' is an erroneous state-ment—there are four . . .

. . . It is not the isolated misdemeanor proving irksome so much as the many—and there are! . . .

. . . Blabber-mouths are scalded . . .

. . . The charge you get is rarely electric . . .

. . . The affinity hot water has for man does not diminish . . .

. . . The holier than thou are unholy in their holiness . . .

. . . American: a person luxuriating in a cocoon which finds itself in a nook on a tree of paradise located in a well-ventilated, temperature-controlled, glass-enclosed, de-weeded hothouse . . .

33

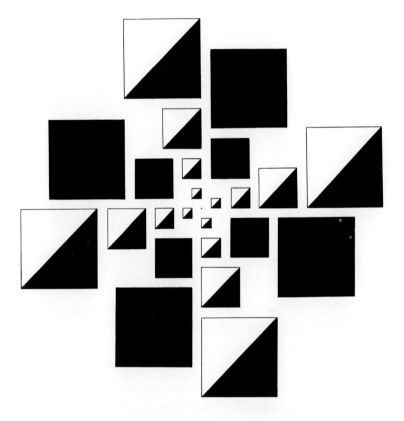

If paired eyes be windows
To your soul so clear,
A scar which lurid shows
Reflects in them with fear.

When minds their truths do hide
From self and brethren all,
A scar far worse inside
Would raise no cloudy pall.

. . . Englishman: a stiff man with a soft interior who speaks the only remaining English . . .

. . . Laughter is as close to tears as love is to hate . . .

. . . Why do people say, "Hah, that's a laugh," to an unfunny matter? . . .

. . . In America gals address each other as 'guys' . . .

. . . Morbidity causes infamy to spread more readily than fame . . .

. . . Everyone is so youth-minded in the new world that even old women call each other 'girls' . . .

. . . A joke is mirth developed on a theme of pain . . .

. . . A way of life is not the life of ways, or is it? . . .

. . . Incidentals clutter the house—incidents our years . . .

. . . Many won't do a damned thing till shown how . . .

. . . Fallacies abound like flies and fester with 'em . . .

. . . ANSWERS ARE IN PURSUIT OF MORE QUESTIONS! . . .

. . . Curiosity seeded learning, after which all hell broke loose . . .

. . . No single manifestation of nature is to blame for our ills. It took two . . .

. . . When one loves, the rest just live . . .

. . . Rape had to predate murder, for 'tis she who places fuel on his fire, and probably did then . . .

. . . We add cruelty to injury . . .

. . . The verb 'to add' is the father of knowledge . . .

. . . Restraint fosters wisdom . . .

. . . The annals of history make mention of from cigarettes, or nothing to mink coats, or queendoms, as costs for the beatific we sully . . .

. . . Genius does what most do not, and does but one, not most . . .

. . . All things indestructible have their specific life-span . . .

. . . Upon the touch of money, a taint; upon its possession, corruption . . .

. . . The most widely fluctuating prices in the world are those for woman . . .

. . . If all else fails, give up . . .

. . . If pride prevents your giving up, take in . . .

. . . Those who speak out sometimes out-speak . . .

. . . The greatest single evil is the drive for procreation. The progeny, if any, are innocent . . .

. . . Guilt is as judges see it . . .

. . . Innocence, per se, belongs in story books . . .

. . . Home: a penitentiary . . .

. . . Suburbia is precisely what the word suggests: below the urban and above the rural . . .

. . . Car: a vehicle of transportation several tons in weight and capable of high speeds which people can't live without and find it difficult to stay alive in . . .

. . . From out of the warmth of incubated coverage and protection comes a stentorian bleating of faith and confidence . . .

. . . Within the realm of sanity there dwells the dormant prehistorian . . .

. . . Disciplinary action merely delays the detonator . . .

. . . Counted sheep don't sleep . . .

. . . Monstrous: that is when a woman can keep the children, the house and the car awarded to her in a divorce, upon remarrying . . .

. . . Bargain: has nothing to do with barter. It is an item strewn across a table in disarray which can be found neatly tucked away under glass with the same price-tag . . .

. . . Band together and lose your remaining identity . . .

. . . The world of the strong has the ideologically conditioned conformist in mind . . .

. . . The simple requirements for remaining young are: 1. avoid photographs of self, 2. shun reflecting surfaces, and 3. stay out of sight. (Caution: strict adherence to all three is essential) . . .

. . . People are kind to memories . . .

. . . Legends are discolored recollections which lose their edges and change their shape with time . . .

. . . Living legends have their dissenters . . .

. . . The socio-economic whip of demand is covertly in the hands of, and cracked by, the so-called weaker sex . . .

. . . The qualifier 'so-called' signifies the speaker's neutrality . . .

. . . Neutralism is insupportable . . .

. . . As well as being a resounding, modern boon credit is the greatest psychological astringent . . .

. . . The modern era's life-expectancy ratio favors the woman . . .

. . . To avoid the alternative of sinking to swimming, don't go near the water . . .

. . . When Sodom was destroyed, all was reclaimed except fulfilled womanhood . . .

. . . Man's ignorance of woman's vacant plight is the volcano he sits on . . .

. . . Greed is the naked nemesis . . .

. . . Paradise is the height and breadth of your body . . .

. . . The pearls of wisdom lie beyond the gates of hell . . .

. . . The reckless are to lava what the prudent are to pumice . . .

. . . Tears do not fill eyes drenched with despair . . .

. . . The farther from your nose the answers are sought, the faster you are running away from yourself . . .

. . . The heat of love will not light a hearth . . .

. . . The deaf really can't hear and as a consequence thereto, are better off . . .

. . . A stitch in time saves nine only after that stitch is sewn . . .

. . . An invention is unique only in its practical application . . .

. . . Any motto is in order if its ends are justified by their means . . .

. . . They say that two heads are better than one. They also say that two cooks spoil the food . . .

. . . A window was designed to give light and to see out. However, some use it to peek in . . .

. . . Altogether too large a faction enjoy the fruits of the few who labor to capitalize on just such enjoyment . . .

. . . Melodrama is to exert oneself in an area of no returns. Comedy is to return for more . . .

Love, that sweet estate
    So unruly,
    Consumes at furious rate
    The unwary.

Hate, that beastly hell
    So translucent,
    Rips viciously as well
    The innocent.

Like, that constant boon
    So touching,
    Never comes too soon
    For clutching.

. . . The need for snap-shots is real clinging to the past . . .

. . . Irony is to pursue the ones who do not want us, and to not want those who pursue us . . .

. . . Possessions are the real ball and chain . . .

. . . The theory of relativity breaks down at the relative of dying, for we know little of the living and nothing of death . . .

. . . Those who are on top of the world forget how it looks at the bottom, or ignore it . . .

. . . Two dissimilar metals and a liquid constitute a battery. Imagine the static charge in a human body with a liquid and all the elements present . . .

. . . Wrath is a draining of bile . . .

. . . The scholar knows a trifle more, and that trifle knows his lack . . .

. . . A greater search divulges a lesser find . . .

. . . The hardest lesson the learned glean is the measure of their scope . . .

. . . Man's sojourn on land masses foreign to him, between the ooze and deep space, is the long and the short of transient . . .

. . . Solve one mystery merely to uncover its baffling progeny . . .

. . . The enshrouding dark lifts but little with light . . .

. . . Prescience would not only sap all strengths—it would also kill all hope . . .

. . . When the facade drops, the animal rears . . .

. . . That inner spark is kept burning by the merciful lack of foreknowledge . . .

. . . Foresight predicts tomorrows destined to be as imperfect as are your todays . . .

. . . If necessity is the mother of invention, then demand is the father of supply . . .

. . . When people say, "It's a matter of life and death," they don't mean the latter, else they would use, or employ, the plural . . .

. . . Publishing houses are pretty grizzly. Each time they cancel a story, or an ad, they initiate a 'kill' . . .

. . . Satisfaction is transient—rarely sufficient . . .

. . . The basic values in life are man's coefficients . . .

. . . Live with and for yourself, for and with others, and find yourself in a statistical minority . . .

. . . The blind canine's nature toward man is one quality to which his master perpetually aspires in vain . . .

. . . A year of gratification ought to be the worth of a hundred spent in non-fulfillment, were it not for insatiable appetites . . .

. . . The simplest thing on earth is imbued with the greatest difficulty of attainment—the art of living . . .

. . . Morality is a fascinating topic of conversation, and that's all it is . . .

. . . Denunciation is defense of a pregnable stand . . .

. . . The moral code is like any other rigidity—very rarely enjoys its solid state . . .

. . . Do more for others than they do for you and accrue interest of a nonfinancial nature resulting in a financial burden . . .

. . . Overtones are misinterpretations. They are the self-oriented concepts of the one colliding with another in the air-space over the hinterland of intolerance . . .

. . . Offspring live in bliss uncaring, and then later care for bliss . . .

. . . If you don't care for these words, try the next . . .

. . . The downtrodden deserve their fate—if they get themself underfoot . . .

. . . The shrewdly deceitful amass wealth, whereas the scrupulously ethical plod . . .

. . . Of all states holy, just one qualifies—your life . . .

. . . Most attempts to please are not merely frustrating and fruitless preoccupations; they are distrusted and suspect . . .

. . . The mute speak volumes . . .

. . . The blooming of the world's largest, loveliest and most fragrant flower, the Victoria Regia, which opens its petals only one night a year, is truly analogous to a man and a woman experiencing ecstasy simultaneously . . .

. . . Crime is spawned in ignorance . . .

. . . Pain is the fertilizer in the soil of pathos; despondency, the lack of rain . . .

. . . The miracle healer knows not the match of sleep . . .

. . . Ignorance, per se, is not necessarily detrimental . . .

. . . Know thyself never . . .

. . . A good loser wishes he was not . . .

. . . Being untrue to others is called, among other things, tact. Being untrue to self is a quality for which no adequate definition exists . . .

. . . A good man is he who decides to laugh last. An exceedingly better one is he who never exercises that prerogative . . .

. . . Sincere gratitude is spoiled when given lip-service . . .

. . . Excuses tread a bog . . .

. . . The pacifist may be more prone to abuse, but he is more durable . . .

. . . The things we shouldn't, or should, do bear no relationship to those undertaken . . .

. . . The greatest strengths entertain thoughts of their every weakness . . .

. . . If mud is opaque, try looking through self . . .

. . . The hurt are hardened, and thus hardened, hurt . . .

. . . A vacuum is abhorred in man as it is by nature . . .

. . . Self-castigation is like suicide, only worse—it lasts much longer . . .

. . . The moment one says 'now' it reverts to 'then' . . .

. . . The burden of proof is seldom on the non-thinker . . .

. . . Declining effect induces cause to withdraw . . .

. . . The pace of time is spaced by events—the longer the strides, the wider the spaces . . .

. . . Defeat can see, but panic is blind . . .

. . . The beginning is gone, the end is upon us. What happened between? . . .

. . . Stimulus and greed are fixed assets on the ledgers of industry . . .

. . . There really isn't any tomorrow, there is only today . . .

. . . A dusking day dawns elsewhere . . .

. . . Youth and wisdom wed but rarely . . .

. . . Power is plagued by chinks in its armor . . .

45

. . . Apologies are automatic reflexes triggered by damage done which is never quite undone . . .

. . . If all ideas are black or white, and neither tint's a color true; then no idea is quite concrete, and stays thus till it water holds . . .

. . . Execution of a threat is the second burden. Issuing the warning was the first . . .

. . . Advice should be taken by its giver . . .

. . . The glow is as warm as the fire . . .

. . . To do what you have, or to have what you did, are the highs and the lows of your life . . .

. . . The only abstraction with tangible merits is one's hard inner core . . .

. . . Apathy is a syndrome which dies when involved . . .

. . . Incompetence eliminates contenders from the rat-race. Does anyone crave a wrenched ankle? . . .

. . . Irrelevancy is the sequel to life . . .

. . . The written words established man's superiority—the spoken ones threaten its foundation . . .

. . . When the expletive 'slut' explodes from one woman, that tongue seldom wags in the orifice of chastity, and usually in the cavity of envy . . .

. . . Gullibility is as guile wishes . . .

. . . The mores of bondage are bonded to lore . . .

. . . The jilted find haven where heaven held reign . . .

. . . The miscast act poorly . . .

. . . The players of roles need pens, not stages . . .

The one who blares, 'Just live for today and to hell with tomorrow,' has no such intention . . .

. . . Derision of errors is not as funny when deriders err . . .

. . . A mother wins battles, and children lose wars . . .

. . . Herd instinct is revealed in the incredible phenomena of the many mindless following the few sightless . . .

. . . If people ever are all that they claim, they could never claim any of what they are . . .

. . . Mental reservations are rusty keys to jammed tongues . . .

. . . The darkest thought will see no light . . .

. . . Misnomers destroy semantics . . .

. . . The prologue to life was scrawled in error, and the text is a compounding of same . . .

. . . Hark to heed the words in song, then watch that bed of roses wilt . . .

. . . Heresey is hearsay . . .

. . . Doctrines are fashioned to suit the many who adapt in public and rebel in private . . .

. . . Rejection seeks refuge in solace implied . . .

. . . Confinement burns with a passion for freedom, whilst freedom has a penchant for confinement . . .

. . . Skillful word-play is like sleight-of-hand . . .

. . . The happy medium is non-existent with perhaps one exception—writing . . .

. . . The stone of 'stupidity' is cast at others making no dent on a carefully guarded stockpile of boulders . . .

. . . When one is victimized by an indiscretion the mistake was exposure in its commission . . .

. . . Variety is not the spice of life, but the necessity . . .

. . . Truth is the originator of fiction . . .

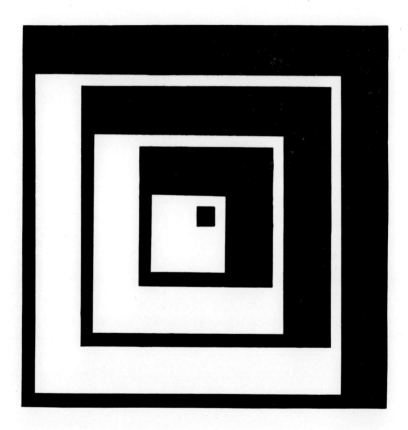

When day of life has breathed

                    Its last

And all things said are wreathed,

                    Are past;

When age and toil has reaped

                    Its wrath

And wage of sin lies heaped

                    On path.

Then do we look to deeds

                    Which shine

And scorn his work which pleads

                    In brine;

Then do we dwell at length

                    With pride.

In all his worth and strengths

                    Abide.

. . . Imposition of will is a movement dreamed up, started and led by the same man . . .

. . . That which weighs nothing and carries much is the human intellect . . .

. . . In the area of specific influence, the relative differentiation between brain and brawn can be derived from that which exists between the elephant and the mouse, respectively, with the same, natural phenomena of psychological fear in the former for the latter manifest . . .

. . . When the spectre of the psyche is raised, all levels of understanding break down, and will continue doing so . . .

. . . In l'affaire d'amour the heart has nothing whatever to do with it. All the excitement is in the mind which, in its overstimulated state, requires more blood from the heart . . .

. . . Love is so blind that even the most homely girl can have a sweet heart, taste notwithstanding . . .

. . . The secret of love refuses to be unlocked . . .

. . . Self-knowledge is the realization that others have higher opinions of yourself than you do, and that belief sustains them . . .

. . . To kill depression, stop all thought . . .

. . . To fight seclusion, be included . . .

. . . Capitalist: a person who spends more than he/she earns . . .

. . . The sentiments of simplicity and eccentricity are entertained by the hermit and the recluse, respectively . . .

. . . The sacred cow is to India as the school bus is to the States . . .

. . . People: a species of biped in quest of answers for which they know not how to ask the questions . . .

. . . Problem: insoluble till admitted . . .

. . . An equation bears a striking resemblance to plain living. Both need a common denominator right and left . . .

. . . The ineffectual and the ruthless, each from diametrically opposed financial camps, yet both impoverished . . .

. . . Mastery of the art of living, per se, engenders emancipation from possessions . . .

. . . If you must imbibe of simplicity, do so in small, measured doses, for it is a heady wine . . .

. . . Reality varies as to perspective, location and vantage point . . .

. . . When you get to a point, you must make your stand, or fall off . . .

. . . A meeting of the minds is insufficient . . .

. . . Weakness wears the stoutest shield . . .

. . . The sea of futility ebbs and floods, disgorging the remnants of shells . . .

. . . The thicker the wall, the greater the need . . .

. . . Cast adrift we bob on the oceans of time without steerage and compass, not even direction . . .

. . . Clearly marked, the road of life bears the legend: NO RETURN . . .

. . . Tenderness, so fragile, can be hurt beyond repair . . .

. . . Time does not ravage—people do. And they leave visible scars . . .

. . . The full worth is never known till it is missed . . .

. . . Selfishness prohibits gratitude, as does pride . . .

. . . Aloneness is the wage of independence . . .

. . . Gratitude is almost always experienced posthumously, and since its recipient is dead, it cannot be reciprocated. Ergo, it doesn't exist . . .

. . . Cats only have one life, and even satisfaction can't imbue them with another . . .

. . . People do, and say, things to be noticed and heard, to justify their existence with others who, yes—have similar requirements . . .

. . . Most persons will do their utmost to outreach themselves, if not others as well, thereby building horizons way into the sky with nary a roof . . .

. . . When love turns to hate, mere touch becomes revolting, and not just one, but both lives, are foundering on the shoals of regret . . .

. . . Once in ruins, emotional quietude can never quite be resurrected . . .

. . . Indulgence, if repelled, is craved when its object is suddenly removed . . .

. . . A canal without traffic is a moving body in which a futile liquid flows to no avail . . .

. . . Warmth of feeling can be chilled with abuse, and with sufficient provocation, will find another nest ere it perishes, or freezes . . .

. . . Givers seek receivers till the latter need no more, then the former live a death . . .

. . . Constitutionally weak; emotionally sick; morally corrupt, and; spiritually confused: This is the animal, Man . . .

. . . 'To thine own self be true' cannot become a reality. For all time, it must remain an ideal . . .

. . . If you do to yourself as you tell others, you'd be more than half-way there . . .

. . . A thing which is sanctioned (countenanced) in some, is crucified in others . . .

. . . Those who climb to dizzy heights, have too far to fall . . .

. . . Millionaire: a man who can only wear one scowl at one time . . .

. . . The ones who have little want to have as much as those who have more, and the latter are also reaching for something. Their daring to speak of happiness is monumental . . .

. . . 40 miles distant nestles your pot of gold. 40 miles in every direction from any spot you occupy—all your livelong days . . .

. . . Look to nightfall with anticipation, and break your fast on bitter fruit . . .

. . . A maxim is wisdom, a parable is deep, a paradox turns on itself and an epigram—? All three! . . .

. . . Conveniences run into white-blood . . .

. . . Be exposed, you are naked. Be unclothed, you are nude. What's the difference? Either way you are vulnerable . . .

. . . Emotion, unfed, lies dormant and barren . . .

. . . Humanity is a headlong, panting dash for the myth which dissipates upon contact . . .

. . . Shangrila is a place like heaven transferred to earth . . .

. . . As ecstasies wane, all miseries rise . . .

. . . An employer looks for qualities in an applicant which he knows exist, and he further knows he does not possess . . .

I die a thousand, tortured deaths,
Each time my words gore deep;
And gasp with choking, rasping breath,
This shame in chagrin steep.
What earthly use all my regret?

I stand impaled and weep.

. . . Many a disillumined beacon luring the hapless voyager to the graveyard of hulks on the shoals of drudgery . . .

. . . Yonder scintillating firmament encrusted with disenchanted unenlightenment . . .

. . . Time shrinks kindness . . .

. . . Speaking out intrudes your presence . . .

. . . Defy convention by adding apples to pears—it is your prerogative . . .

. . . The slightest pain defeats the greatest joy . . .

. . . Longing is nothing more, or less, than selfish avariciousness . . .

. . . Memory favors affronts . . .

. . . Moral codes are in jeopardy each time the accidental seed vanquishes reluctant fertility . . .

. . . A hue and cry is a red herring . . .

. . . Licit, or illicit, bones in the closets of society which tramples on the latter . . .

. . . Back becomes front if one turned that way . . .

. . . The meeting of husband and spouse would be as historic as the touching of one's right elbow by the right hand on the same arm . . .

. . . When bodies don't need sleep, people force the issue by counting sheep . . .

. . . Touch another deeply once and it may be the vanguard of many . . .

. . . When someone says 'Everything happens for the best,' it's a resignation to fate, rather than a shaping of it . . .

. . . Passion stalks stimulus . . .

. . . Dilemma is the case against the man who will not abstain from woman, yet lives in hope to wed a virgin . . .

. . . Dispatching a killer to the promised land will not wrench his victim thence . . .

. . . The blood-bespattered gashes in the pages of time shall never mellow, and shan't ever heal, however illustrious the cause . . .

. . . Taking morbid, ghoulish pleasure in any 'just' retribution perpetrated on a fellow creature, is bringing another segment of man's inhumanity to man come starkly, crashing home . . .

. . . Clothes which conceal shame are the wafer-thin, top layers of oblivious decadence . . .

. . . Steal reason without, and reason steals within . . .

. . . Prudes retreat to ivory towers where they shed their sterilized tears in self-pity . . .

. . . Assuage hunger ere it cannibalizes . . .

. . . Whence it goeth, thence it cometh . . .

. . . 'What goes up, must come down' is really a time-worn statement which wore out after the Venus and Mars probes . . .

. . . Should you wish all fear were shed, then would you wish a shed in fear . . .

. . . The stronghold of social pressure holds a strangled court . . .

. . . Along came the clique—up sprang the snob . . .

. . . The virtuous enjoy diminishing limelight . . .

. . . Inspiration is never pulled from a hat . . .

. . . Lost youth laments the loss of moisture behind its ear . . .

. . . When time barters youth for age, neither side really has an edge, though youth feels cheated . . .

. . . Altogether too little mental agility abets physical feebleness . . .

. . . The love of your heart is not the heart of your love . . .

. . . Man may govern the stars, but never without emotions to govern him . . .

. . . The constraining talons of well-intentioned parenthood hound an offspring's jugular vein to its grave . . .

. . . Dehydration of spontaneity ushers in senility . . .

. . . Sleeping is a sampling of dying . . .

. . . The theme of the ages pulses with the struggle for survival . . .

. . . Unrequited, naked ghosts haunt most psyches so desolate, wailing not because they bleed, but bemoaning needed rest . . .

. . . If, out of the depths of your consciousness, you must feel sorry, favor the living. The dead need no such grace . . .

. . . The truly emancipated scramble not for attainment . . .

. . . The shadow of the image of man, far afield pursuing a niche fitted for itself, instead of calmly urging his image to settle into the niche for which he is fitted . . .

. . . So long as mankind has what it doesn't want, and wants what it had and threw away, so long will peace be a myth . . .

. . . Irrefutable proof is the sealer of fates . . .

. . . The event disproving the lure as well as the cache, would also be the last . . .

. . . Rob man of choice and you kill the dream . . .

. . . Preferences exercise controls . . .

. . . The feuding between abstract and extract has only one outcome—the former prevails . . .

. . . Actions to decide followed by decisions to act, are the precursors of pressure . . .

. . . When you are undecided, don't . . .

. . . Doubt conducts the orchestra of ignorance in the ritual music of uncertainty, composed by rationalization . . .

. . . Heed your dictates . . .

. . . Remembrance is a stranger in the land of Id . . .

. . . Avocation is rarely vocation . . .

. . . Liking what you do is not always doing what you like . . .

. . . Limits have none . . .

. . . Glance at your legs and muse their behavior when you must stand and deliver . . .

. . . The foibles of the human race are the fables of note . . .

. . . Those who say where they might have gone but for the grace of God, are still looking back . . .

. . . Retrospection softens the event reviewed . . .

. . . Of all concepts available, self is most flattered . . .

. . . Charity starts within oneself, not at home, and then rarely in its true form . . .

. . . The one who has experienced the pinnacle, also knows the pit . . .

. . . The ultimate candor is unbiased insight . . .

. . . The price of righteousness is exorbitant . . .

. . . Stoicism is transparent. It can be pierced . . .

. . . The world is not so much what you made it. It is more what the world makes of you . . .

. . . The one way to look at life and survive is through rose-colored lenses . . .

. . . Discipline is regimentation of the mind . . .

. . . Short-sightedness is not solely of the eyes . . .

. . . Those who refuse—withdraw . . .

. . . Of all the powers we have, few have it over observation and none are less costly . . .

. . . Argumentation is defensiveness, or a semantic breakdown . . .

. . . Differences of opinion are crutches. They tend to support one's individuality . . .

. . . Anger is subjectivity replacing objectivity. It is like tears, cleanses your system . . .

. . . If your true self you are afraid to expose, don't get angry or drunk . . .

. . . Pigeons are not the only things which are holed . . .

. . . Will-power without determination is like a ship without a rudder; without enthusiasm, a stagnant force . . .

. . . Trust your emotions implicitly, for they are yours. Be wary of second thoughts, these are not . . .

. . . A mind weighed down by self-imprisonment turns on itself, or cracks . . .

. . . Cause without effect is like dreams without reality . . .

. . . Of all the motive forces, ambition ranks high . . .

. . . Withdrawal is reflex action which lost its sense of direction . . .

. . . Man is filed along with documents . . .

. . . Everyone is working, even when they are resting . . .

. . . Contentment deprives the self-satisfied of purpose . . .

. . . Uneasy rests the crown on the head of the best . . .

. . . Rules and regulations are for the conformist; true independence and individualism is reserved for the strong . . .

. . . Faith moves mountains, but confidence shapes the world . . .

. . . Life isn't all that precious, except one's own . . .

. . . Vehemence encounters resistance; adamance engenders opposition; fanaticism is denied the grace of rejection . . .

. . . The cruelest of tortures is mental . . .

. . . A death of one mind is a loss to the world . . .

. . . The sword is strong; the pen more so; whilst oratory has them both vanquished . . .

. . . Loyalty varies as to the purse strings . . .

. . . There are scores of ways to live one's life—one's own, though, should suffice . . .

. . . Everything wrong is right, and everything right is wrong . . .

. . . A diseased mind could be the liberated . . .

. . . If you want to hide, don't be a hermit. Try keeping your mouth shut . . .

. . . Uncountable the roads which lead away from Rome . . .

. . . Those who 'will,' succeed at anything . . .

. . . Hitch your wagon to a star, load it with ambition, and you're blessed with a life-long romance . . .

1.

A drive,

A need,

A thought

    In quest.

2.

A deed,

A gasp,

A bliss

    With zest.

3.

A time,

A wait,

A care

    Through rest.

4.

A bed,

A fear,

A groan

    At best.

5.

A birth,

A slap,

A breath

    To test.

6.

A cry,

A child,

A crib

    Does nest.

7.

A pride,

A man,

A life

    Of jest.

. . . Any falsehood is true to some . . .

. . . The word 'absolutely' is precisely that . . .

. . . The ultimate insult accorded the fanatic is silence . . .

. . . Rest is a hard commodity to come by; it is neither here nor there . . .

. . . One truth is hard to take; truths more often, are brutal; truth continually is completely demoralizing . . .

. . . Should you be out to confuse the world, be honest . . .

. . . Absolute power, if such a thing were possible, would have a humbling effect. It is the near, imperfect kind which poses all the danger . . .

. . . A truism is not true to all . . .

. . . Vengeance when wrought by the meek, is more devastating than any . . .

. . . Populate your day with pleasantries and these will invest your life . . .

. . . Honor is translated into coin, and reduced by the lack of it . . .

. . . Human madness knows no end, but grandeur does . . .

. . . Vindictiveness is vaingloriousness. It is the mark of the immature . . .

. . . 'How is the world treating you?' Exactly as you treat it . . .

. . . The rate at which people reproduce is proportionate to the rapidity with which they forget how to live . . .

. . . Sanity is relative to affluence . . .

. . . Envy is little less than avarice. Breeds resentment . . .

. . . The intelligentsia criticizes the moron for lacking the thing he had a potential for . . .

. . . It takes all sorts to make a world, but only a handful can keep it together, whatever the result . . .

. . . Apathy is a relinquishing voice of the masses to the deceptively solicitous purr of the select . . .

. . . Help should be begged for to do any good . . .

. . . Expletives expend mental power, let alone waste words . . .

. . . Terror is an awful thing, though it hardens one's mettle . . .

. . . Originality comes with sophistication . . .

. . . The quest is more necessary than the goal . . .

. . . Discontentment is a relentless task-master . . .

. . . Save the other's neck, you're a hero. Save your own and there will be someone who's disappointed . . .

. . . Money has to come from some source, ergo: the susceptible are elected . . .

. . . Poverty strikes the victim of circumstance as it does the unimaginative . . .

. . . Beauty is in the word, the rest is in the mind . . .

. . . Courage is either blind, or 'dutch.' In either case, it is to be admired . . .

. . . Practically all accomplishments of a failure are discounted . . .

. . . Those who are less aware, are more fortunate . . .

. . . Creativity is born in strife . . .

. . . Achievement of an undertaking has the explicable habit of leaving us disenchanted . . .

. . . Bottled fury is like a capped volcano . . .

. . . Those who sweep a nation, wield a large broom . . .

. . . Vulnerability craves succor . . .

. . . Attention is best filled by the opposite sex . . .

. . . Say 'opposite sex,' and you segregate . . .

. . . Succor needs attention . . .

. . . Those who segregate—discriminate, which fans the battle of the sexes . . .

. . . When the sexes declare a truce, the bottom will drop out of rubber. And when peace is established, news media will fold . . .

. . . Adulation is symbolism. Faith is a fetish. Both are synonymous with frailty . . .

. . . Assent, you are a yes-man. Negate, you are a cynic. Do neither and you are a bore . . .

. . . Turnabout is a farewell to recklessness . . .

. . . There isn't a soul one can rely on, your own included . . .

. . . Divine guidance is to man what the blind is to the mute. The latter can direct the former, but hardly the reverse . . .

. . . Most transgressions are forgiven the successful . . .

. . . To make money does not require brains so much as ruthlessness . . .

. . . The vicious should not lay sole claim to ruthlessness . . .

. . . Utter the word 'henceforth' and you are looking ahead, temporarily . . .

. . . One who laughs last gives way to vindictiveness . . .

. . . One would suppose the pleasures of the flesh to be more intense; with all due gratitude to our prudes . . .

. . . The word 'sex' is not feared, but the consequential connotation is . . .

. . . Sex is dead; long live sex . . .

. . . The least costly are given most stintingly . . .

. . . The most expensive is not necessarily the best, but the scarcest . . .

. . . To say 'it never fails' is as bad as 'its human nature' . . .

. . . Hoorah for noise . . .

. . . If anyone gives you a pain, you need a doctor . . .

. . . Theology is linked to sex. Before you say 'pish-posh' look for tell-tale rosettes in stained-glass windows in churches and on ladies' lingerie . . . .

. . . Philosophy envelopes everything—metes out opinionated strata embracing creation . . .

. . . Hindsight is always simpler than foresight, which is why we have class-distinction . . .

. . . Theorize, and dream. Practice, and live . . .

. . . Retrospection aids introspect. To coin the missing link, let us repair to the mint for: 'EXTROSPECT' . . .

. . . Hypocrisy is the cardinal sin . . .

. . . The scope of any statement is determined by its carrying power . . .

. . . Predetermination is pure conjecture . . .

. . . Pulling something apart is easy. Putting it back together again takes time, if possible . . .

. . . Deception is a crime unto self . . .

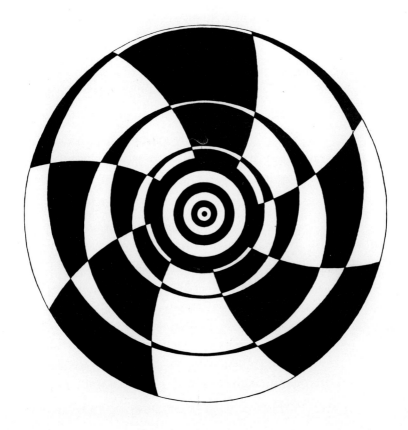

The heaven's vault, a purplish black,
Its passage end, it must;
The risen sun its hold will crack
To warm the night-chilled crust.

A trembling gray, then lighter shades,
Thus orange emanates.
The dark is vanquished, quickly fades;
Hot sun scintillates.

The sky a blazing red and gold
As life stirs dreamily.
Gone are myriad stars untold,
Our pace resuming giddily.

A different day is really here,
Resolves anew we spawn.
The past is gone, the future near,
No present but the dawn.

. . . There are many qualms for the courageous, because they know fear and wished they didn't . . .

. . . In all of man's endeavors, the path seems clear toward his destiny, though his destiny will remain unclear . . .

. . . Save yourself if you must, but solely at your own expense . . .

. . . The demise of the one makes a little more room for another, temporarily . . .

. . . People will succeed at every*thing*, with emphasis on the last syllable. As for all three? They can try . . .

. . . No sooner does one say 'never' and the thing is done . . .

. . . Ask, and thou shalt get, so howl . . .

. . . People without foundations are like buildings without that vital property . . .

. . . Freedom in thinking, the open quest, is usually unshackled . . .

. . . Not everyone loves a parade . . .

. . . Cliches may weaken in their impact. Their words never do . . .

. . . Sightless minds cannot be helped . . .

. . . Love is the result of desire . . .

. . . All roads through Plato lead to bed. When they don't, the journey ends . . .

. . . A mind in flight is a heart encased . . .

. . . Understanding would vanquish bigotry . . .

. . . Empathy would unite the world—so, let us cross off unity . . .

. . . 'Every action has an equal and opposite reaction.' Therein lies our problem . . .

. . . Those who shut out, lock in . . .

. . . 'No man is an island'; spoken from the haven of lonely desolation . . .

. . . A hovel can be home beyond mansions, and often is . . .

. . . Try, try again, and break your back! . . .

. . . To be indecent is to luxuriate . . .

. . . The discards of the one are the treasures of another . . .

. . . Nothing, not the slightest thing, is meaningless . . .

. . . Words which aren't vehicles for thought have not been uttered. Why then do we collide with so much thinking afoot? . . .

. . . When self-love is publicly sanctioned, many minds will file for divorce from as many of their hearts . . .

. . . We find all save that most sought . . .

. . . Sex isn't everything. However, that which is better is unknown, though one may trust people to look for it . . .

. . . Truth runs the entire gamut . . .

. . . The road you are on is seldom the one covertly desired . . .

. . . The surf booms, hear it or not . . .

. . . Long after the clocks ticked their last, time will advance . . .

. . . If we all danced to someone's tune, this world would be crawling with dancers, let alone musicians . . .

. . . The term 'poor' is not necessarily applied to the poverty-stricken. The unfortunates get their slice of it . . .

. . . Of all tolls paid, keen intellect extracts the heaviest . . .

. . . Be aware and know misery . . .

. . . Whatever one does seems wrong . . .

. . . "Well, I'll be," from people too timid to add the fourth word . . .

. . . We cannot live with others, and we cannot live with ourselves. Suggestions, anyone? . . .

. . . Every man is basically alone, especially in a crowd . . .

. . . Decay of the moral fiber is seeded by unschooled sex . . .

. . . The unusual is nothing more than the unfamiliar . . .

. . . Every man for himself, for himself, for himself . . .

. . . Time is the final victor . . .

. . . Escapisms we know, oblivion we don't . . .

. . . Dispel your mists and expose those truths . . .

. . . Man hath no peace till death, and then? . . .

. . . Beauty is as the eye sees it, but not till it is stressed . . .

. . . Being transcends ugliness . . .

. . . Beauty is its own jailer . . .

. . . Disseminating the gene may throw *some* light on the complexities of life, whilst the enigma of man endures secure . . .

. . . For anything to have less appeal, all it needs is to be practiced, or partaken of, more . . .

. . . Loneliness is real peace, if you can stand it . . .

. . . Two plus two equals a different four for all . . .

. . . One would be utterly unnerved if heaven did forbid . . .

. . . We are nice to but a few . . .

. . . With all of its debris, how can fire cleanse? . . .

. . . Contradictions are the termites of the fibre . . .

. . . The reason kindness can kill is because we do not get enough of it . . .

. . . 'Never the twain shall meet' is truer for man and woman than for east and west. He may take but one and win; she can take a thousand and fail . . .

. . . A substitute profanity lightens but little . . .

. . . If we had to walk on thin ice each time a ticklish subject came along, we'd either laugh ourselves to death, or drown. Perhaps we are . . .

. . . The first is seldom that, and the last never is . . .

. . . If others make you sick to your stomach, you may have constipation . . .

. . . A horse of a different color is no horse at all . . .

. . . Mind and body mated—that is the dearth . . .

. . . As much as we are kicked in our teeth, still do we bite off more and chew the cud thereafter . . .

. . . The imbued allow for little, admit less, and give nothing . . .

. . . Don't dismiss what is imagined, and muddle through with eyes unseeing . . .

. . . Look about you carefully. See anything? Sure? Now, blast you, look again! . . .

. . . Ego-worship, from cradle to grave . . .

. . . The nearest thing to a bottomless pit is the stomach . . .

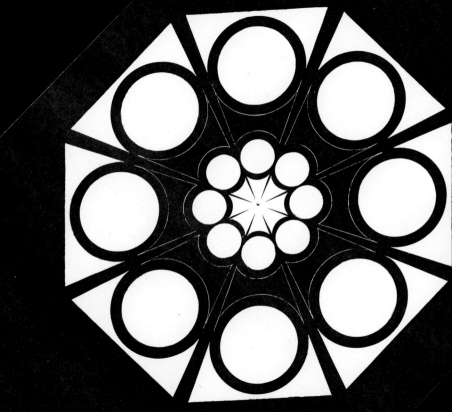

Primeval art thou gnawing curse
Thou spectre called: just sustenance;
Wouldst one's reason thence disburse,
Thou scepter whence no abstinence.

1

        The elements dictate a sheath
        So needfully in raiment;
2
        Tho' 'tis the other shame beneath
        Of fear which governs dominant.

'Tis then that privacy and greed
Caused man to seek out shelter.
Therein he shuts himself to bl⁄ ⌐d
Confusement in a welter.

3

        As nature coursed through lethargy
        And quickened pulse found music,
4
        His spirit burned in effigy
        With flesh of earth intrinsic.

To know life's whys and all wherefors
Would pose his first prerequisite.
This knowledge gives not up its stores;
Could make your days too exquisite.

5

. . . Specialization enslaved the taste buds, and these in turn victimized the purse . . .

. . . There is only one element which will continue to defy mathematics—the human . . .

. . . No two females are dissimilar to a hungered man . . .

. . . Meetings are like parades, they depersonalize . . .

. . . Clapping is a barbaric echo of prehistoric times. Now try depriving the performer of it . . .

. . . The cynic pokes ridicule at everything. The satirist capitalizes on it . . .

. . . Plod, and they are feet of clay. Run, and they have wings. Do neither, and you are gone . . .

. . . Disagreement is to be encouraged; it helps stave off boredom, perhaps even stagnation . . .

. . . Than the ego, no greater. Than the Id, no equal . . .

. . . A wrongdoing hurts the wrongdoer the most . . .

. . . Everyone has a conscience, sooner or later . . .

. . . True selflessness is a myth . . .

. . . Realism is relative, materialism is universal, idealism is little understood, yet people kill one another for any one of the three . . .

. . . Intellect is either inherent, or acquired. Neither does the subject good unless exercised . . .

. . . The term 'ultimate' is farcical . . .

. . . Fence-straddling robs one of ground to stand on . . .

. . . Strife is what you make it, not what you say it is . . .

. . . The two chronic results of 'fun' are hangovers and offspring . . .

. . . 'Peace on earth and good will to man'—with strings attached . . .

. . . The many who can't are led by the few who can, competent or not . . .

. . . Attitudes are ships. Negative ones founder whilst positive ones deliver their manifest . . .

. . . An opinion is considered, estimated, or unfounded—never humble . . .

. . . Mind is riches beyond wealth . . .

. . . Abandonment is the better part of pride . . .

. . . Nature regales resplendent . . .

. . . Specific opportunity is the missing ingredient in wrecked lives . . .

. . . Injustice comes through shortsightedness . . .

. . . Beauty does as others wish . . .

. . . Smiles disarm . . .

. . . The masochistic nature of man is such that if punishment were abolished, crime would reduce, might even vanish . . .

. . . The babble you hear are tongues. Language is for the purpose of semantics . . .

. . . The easiest answers solve the most difficult problems . . .

. . . Where everything is important, nothing is trivial; every facet, every segment, every phase . . .

. . . Self-imposed and most rigid is the code of ethics embraced by the non-believer . . .

. . . The unafraid are in trouble . . .

. . . The power women hold over men is the weakest link between them . . .

. . . No one is all right—unto himself . . .

. . . The fascination women have for men is the ace in the hole, but the possessiveness therein thins it out . . .

. . . You lose your job—"C'est la vie"
Your house burns down—"C'est la vie"
The wife leaves you—"C'est la vie"
When you die—"C'est finis" . . .

. . . Human attractions are fleeting things . . .

. . . Familiarity breeds children . . .

. . . Ennui is drowned in drink and is resurrected for more of either, or both . . .

. . . Ardor flowers during spring . . .

. . . Be a male, win a girl; be a man, win respect . . .

. . . Sex is both the state and the act. Both are little understood . . .

. . . The conflicting misconceptions regarding homosapien functions smash themselves to smithereens against basic wantonness . . .

. . . No matter where you go, or how far, the bridge to the caves will stand . . .

. . . A brain of any kind, is dangerous. A lucid brain is lethal. The host of a brilliant mind devours itself . . .

. . . If there were a third sex the primordial may long have been shed, if the earth were still spinning . . .

. . . Inspiration springs from a fertilized mind . . .

. . . The what was evidenced, the how robs one of breath, the why is beyond us . . .

. . . Weeping arouses sympathy, and delineation begets an affinity . . .

. . . The sexes dove-tail so perfectly by being what they are without having to work at it. It is by striving valiantly, so desperately to mesh that they move apart perforce . . .

. . . Spatial reference points are the cradles of discord . . .

. . . Say "This," and they'll say, "That?" Ah well, no one agrees . . .

. . . You think, therefore you are. "What?" . . .

. . . The instant you deem to have it made—stop! . . .

. . . Expecting the romance of first love to continue through wedlock would be asking for too much . . .

. . . Fealty is the harp plucked by incompetent woman . . .

. . . The dual standard is not mutually sanctioned . . .

. . . Stop—and you have really had it . . .

. . . Notoriety is sought to establish an identity. Any sort at all . . .

. . . Man happens to pensive woman . . .

. . . The compliment in flattery is veiled desire . . .

. . . Puttering is better than languishing . . .

. . . Fatherhood is the worth of all his worldly possessions . . .

. . . The everlasting mystery of pregnancy and birth reduces the man to malleable consistency in the equally perplexed, but uncomplaining, hands of woman . . .

. . . To be wanted—want . . .

. . . Hate boomerangs . . .

. . . To watch a band-wagon dwindle, dislike it . . .

. . . Naturalness preceded the cave . . .

. . . Teetotalers can be found on, or off, wagons . . .

. . . You are born, you live, then you die. The first and last are no trouble; it is that which comes between the two taxing one's patience and fortitude so illimitably . . .

. . . Purity must be tuned, as does a piano . . .

. . . The worn facade is like an air-castle of brittle glass . . .

. . . Of the traits which are foreign, candor is mentioned . . .

. . . What you do, or did, is not as the world knows it . . .

. . . A first taste reduces the next . . .

. . . A parried glance anticipates the carnal . . .

. . . Riddance of an annoyance leaves a void . . .

. . . The dark secret magnifies, or festers. Why not air it? . . .

. . . Honor is the step-child of aspiration . . .

. . . The equation of the sexes elludes solubility, not because it doesn't exist, but because few apply it, or themselves . . .

. . . Existence equals Marriage multiplied by the square of Compatibility . . .

. . . Purity is as purity does not . . .

. . . People with stars in their eyes are in the dark . . .

. . . The only instants in a person's life where a searing, single-mindedness of purpose is exercised, occurs during the heat of the love-act . . .

. . . Sex lived till it died at the hands of the puritans . . .

. . . People who make many fine points each day, go through a lot of pencils . . .

. . . The world has no place for the sick . . .

. . . Pity and sympathy only serve to drive the recipient further into despair . . .

Brushes stir intrinsic whorls
On canvas in shades warm;
Dancing bristles dab in swirls
Of oils in depth and form.

The painter stabs with vivid lines
To patterns round, or straight;
Steely blues and ruby wines
Until such hues would mate.

Color in an ochre riot
Dazzles up alive;
Captured in artistic fiat
Through a flashing drive.

Daubing on a clashing trace
In vermilion dark;
Shadings at the subject base
All creators mark.

Skies and lakes in cobalt ice
So brilliantly aglow;

Amber sets and rises spice
The beauty and the flow.

Maroons and browns in sombre lots
Shroud a thought in gloom;
Deeper tints in other spots
On horizons loom.

Hints of grass and foliage green
Blend a vibrant tone
Nature's pictures so serene,
Real, unspoiled and lone.

Paintings at the master's hand
Wait for famished eyes;
Searching through the ageless sand
Where creation lies.

Doors thrown open to the soul
By a masterpiece;
Reaches out to spark a coal
In undying peace.

. . . The advice you got, you needn't have . . .

. . . The pathos of humankind is a horde of zombies on the march they know not why, nor where . . .

. . . Bitterness washes not away with tears . . .

. . . Provision insulates against despair . . .

. . . An accurate yard-stick of a culture is its music . . .

. . . From giants to mice in nothing flat . . .

. . . The individualist is a foreigner in collectivisms . . .

. . . Groups stifle freedom . . .

. . . Loyalties go to the highest bidder . . .

. . . A counter-spy plays both ends against the middle . . .

. . . People either preach, gossip, or chatter. Very basic. Everyone has something to say . . .

. . . Less progress—more earthiness . . .

. . . Eros has a seat in every gene . . .

. . . Talent is given where credence is due . . .

. . . Forked tongues do better in cheek . . .

. . . The sole distributor of air, were it sold, would own the world . . .

. . . How to succeed in business without crossing the Styx prematurely . . .

. . . Take away all writing instruments and observe progress grind to a halt . . .

. . . Conservatists cling to that vestige of sanity . . .

. . . Dreams either spring from, or become, reality . . .

. . . A trust is placed at your own risk . . .

. . . New Year's resolutions dissipate like clouds . . .

. . . Looking before jumping may change your mind . . .

. . . The beginning is what the end made it . . .

. . . Unprecedented candor is a frank statement of fact by a woman to her man that she and ecstasy are strangers . . .

. . . Women prefer to be needed primarily for themselves. Sex is pleasurably incidental . . .

. . . His precipitous impatience is her enigmatic inconsistency . . .

. . . A thief's victim has the advantage which the latter seldom exploits . . .

. . . Entertained thoughts spill through inadvertent lips . . .

. . . Sentiment in abeyance craves expression . . .

. . . Antidisestablishmentarianistically . . .

. . . His unschooled, animalistic illusions are her sub-conscious, heart-rending disillusionments . . .

. . . Doubt a good portion of what you see, more of what you read, and everything you hear . . .

. . . Harbinger: a lingering whiff of perfume assailing a man's nostrils, tantalizing his over-active imagination . . .

. . . Romanticism is incurable . . .

. . . That which *surely* is, can not be . . .

. . . Female finality is a male's interlude—the sacrificial lamb of chastity offered Adonis on the altar of passion without redemption . . .

. . . Men are callous, unfeeling brutes bent on a destructive course of self-gratification at the expense of enduringly long-suffering maternity . . .

. . . Ink is to people what mortar is to bricks . . .

. . . The illumined cast no shadow . . .

. . . Irrationality is weaned on bosoms of failure . . .

. . . Depth is the extent of comprehension . . .

. . . Some there are with both feet planted firmly on the ground. Many there are who wish to fly; these latter are still up there . . .

. . . Constancy is a discipline of love . . .

. . . Words handed down are thoughts immortalized . . .

. . . Isolationism is an aphrodisiac spiced with narcissus . . .

. . . Deprived of the adulation she was conditioned to expect, Venus would crumble . . .

. . . Pan drinketh of the elixir which lifteth him above the commons . . .

. . . Resplendently sedate foliage contemplates verdant humankind . . .

. . . Grecian philosophy adorns the crags with a mosaic of wisdom . . .

. . . The only comical aspect of nature deservant of the distinction is man's insupportable concept of 'pleasure' . . .

. . . The mended knows its fault . . .

. . . A stench is not a smell till noses twitch . . .

. . . The beckoning fingers of Midas lure on . . .

. . . The touch from beyond the grave is belated conscience . . .

. . . Boredom knows of much to do and little to excite . . .

. . . Forts at war with fortresses are separated by unbridgeable moats . . .

. . . Wrestled problems are two things: walked away from or mangled . . .

. . . 'Schadenfreude' is international . . .

. . . Downgrading recoils . . .

. . . Ideas never die . . .

. . . Antecedents beget successors . . .

. . . Embellishment emphasizes prerogative . . .

. . . The alien in your midst has his peculiarly unalienable
right also, though it sits in your craw . . .

. . . Goaded feelings erupt in your face . . .

. . . Civilization gave us 'joy' to contend with . . .

. . . Escape your heritage never . . .

. . . The apple lies in sight of its tree . . .

. . . Run till you drop, and come full circle . . .

. . . Perception is a light thrusting through that chink . . .

. . . Lyrics are the satire of life, and their message the cold
fact . . .

. . . Martyrdom glorifies death . . .

. . . The Silver Chalice and the Holy Grail are the cups
which once brimmeth over . . .

. . . Hopelessness is smothered . . .

. . . Shadows should be boxed . . .

. . . The multiplicity of tranquility is a multiple of simplicity . . .

. . . The origin of poppycock is fascinating . . .

. . . A tomboy has her fair share of male hormones . . .

. . . The past, as we know it, and a time machine, would
clash on first contact . . .

. . . Where feet are shod, they once were webbed . . .

. . . To savor life, just flirt with death . . .

. . . The quickened pulse thrills to the committed wrong . . .

. . . The roots of time are untapped . . .

. . . Music brooks no argument . . .

. . . Misses strike harder than hits . . .

. . . Much of what is bottled bears no label . . .

. . . Trends toward simple beginnings gain momentum in dynamic societies . . .

. . . The aftermath of suppression is repressed . . .

. . . Ideas sown in the loam of minds can be reaped by pen in a harvest of gems . . .

. . . At midnight yesterday becomes tomorrow, and tomorrow became today . . .

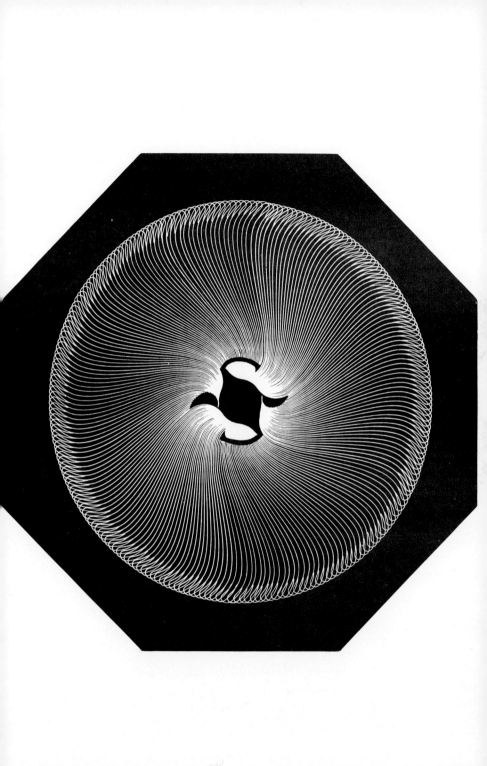

With scarce a seed,

    With less to plough,

        With naught to toil;

            The end arrives.

Then mind will breed,

    Then thought does bow

        Then words take soil;

            Beginning thrives.

A sequel is more of a different same.

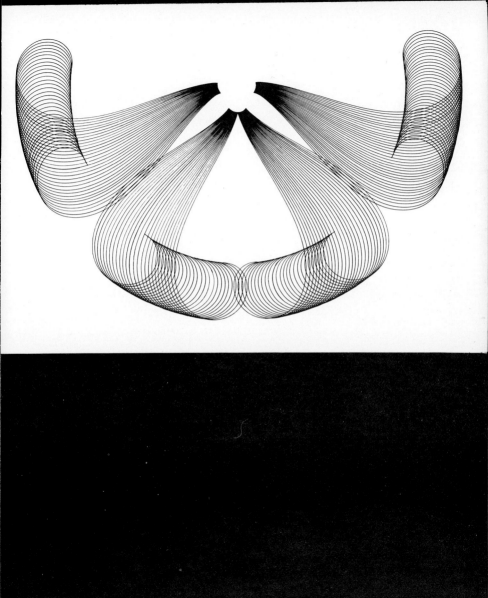

EPILOGUE

An epilogue may be a dying, last gasp to an epic eulogy, or soliloquy. To the author, however, it bears overtones of an epitaph.

Sufficient unto this book are the epigrams thereof.

FRED J. SINGER